AmericanGirl Library®

# christmas
# crafts

American Girl®

It's
time to
deck the **halls**,
try a **yummy** treat,
create the perfect gift,
wrap a **package** that's **sweet**.
It's all inside, with lots of help, too,
to make the **joys** and dreams of Christmas
come true
for
you!

Art Direction and Design: Camela Decaire

Production: Kendra Pulvermacher, Mindy Rappe

Tabletop Photography: Bob Esparza, Dave Jordano, Radlund Photography, Mark Salisbury, Mike Walker

Model Photography: Raphael Buchler, Thomas Heinser, Dave Jordano, Sandy May

Stylists: Tricia Doherty, Camela Decaire,
Jessica Hastreiter, Trula Magruder, Kendra Pulvermacher, Kristi Thom

Illustrations: Geri Bourget

Library of Congress Cataloging-in-Publication Data
available on request.

# table of contents

# getting started

## important!

Please read through the directions carefully. The supplies you'll need are marked in colored type. Be sure to gather all supplies before you begin!

Always **ask an adult to help you** when you see this hand  or when you feel a project is a bit hard to do yourself.

Be sure to cover your work area with **newspapers** when using paint, glue, or glitter. Always keep paint, scissors, and other craft supplies **out of reach** of little kids.

## glues

Always use **craft glue** unless a project mentions another kind. Craft glue cleans up easily with water—so don't use it if you think your project will ever need to be washed!

**Glitter glue** is much like craft glue only it's sparkly when it dries.

**Jewel glue** or **fabric glue** works well when applying gems or glitter to fabric. Usually, these glues can be washed, but read the glue label to be sure it says "washable."

## microbeads

**Microbeads** are so tiny, they don't have holes. To apply these beads, use an **adhesive microbead tape or paper.** If the paper or tape isn't holding your beads very well, apply a coat of craft glue over the beads with a small paintbrush.

# getting started

## jewelry

For large beading projects, you'll save time and trouble if you buy **hanks of beads** rather than stringing beads yourself. A "hank" is a bundle of strung beads. Before a project, untie the bundle, separate the strands, and tie 3 knots on the end of each strand, so that beads won't slip off strings.

## glitters

You can find a variety of glitters in craft stores—from **large glitter squares** to **micro glitters** that are as fine as sand. For fabric designs, be sure the glitter label says "washable."

## where to find it

For the items listed below, these stores are your best bet:

### Craft store
- adhesive microbead paper or tape
- beads • candy melts • cork sheets
- craft wire • Fimo clay • glycerine soap • jewelry findings • jingle bells
- microbeads • oil-based candy flavorings • paper clay • paper punches
- paraffin wax • pliers • rhinestones or gems • shells or starfish • soap glitter
- soap scent • Styrofoam balls

### Health food store
- coconut oil (beauty department)

### Office supply store
- double-sided tape • pushpins

# so simple

**Making gifts for friends and family is as easy as 1-2-3!**

## 'tis the *season*

Decorate a tree with treasures from the sea. **Shells**
and **starfish** glimmer when painted with **glitter glue.**
Apply glue to both sides with a **paintbrush.** Let dry.
Cross ends of a short loop of **ribbon,** and glue them flat
to top backside. Let dry before hanging.

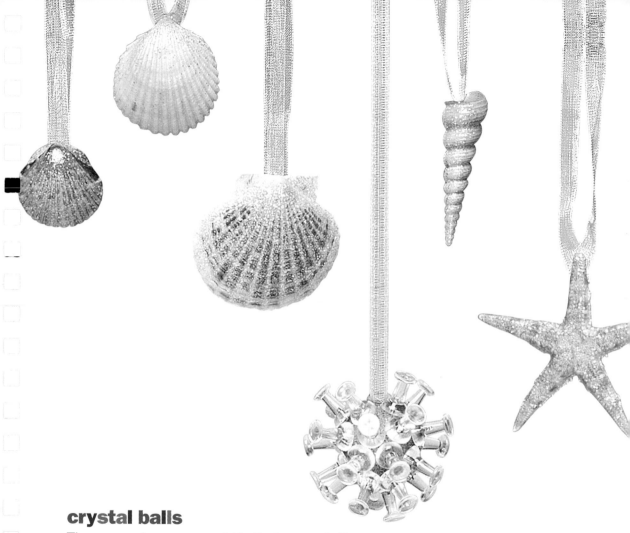

## crystal balls

These unusual ornaments twinkle like ice crystals. Press **clear pushpins** into a plain or painted **Styrofoam ball**. To hang, add **craft glue** to a pushpin point, and press a **ribbon** into ball. Let dry.

## oh, christmas tee!

Decorate your tee with fabric glue and rhinestones. Slide **wax paper** inside a **T-shirt**. Lightly draw a design on shirt in **pencil.** (See page 63 for patterns.) For a candy cane, fill in outlines with **fabric glue,** then press on **rhinestones** in a striped pattern. Let dry. For a tree, fill in outlines with glue, then cover design with **glitter.** Let dry 24 hours. Tap off extra glitter. Glue on **beads** or rhinestones as ornaments. Let dry for another day.

## silent lights

Press colorful **metallic stickers** on glass **candle-holders** for a gift that shimmers and shines.

## stars of wonder

All you need are glitter and glue to make these sparkly stars. Draw a star on a piece of **paper,** then lay it on a **rimmed cookie sheet.** Place **wax paper** over star, and trace design with a thick line of **fabric glue.** Completely cover glue with **glitter.** Let dry for 24 hours. Tap off extra glitter over cookie sheet, then gently pull star from wax paper. Tie on **ribbon** or **cord.**

13

## snowy sweets

Sift snowy shapes onto store-bought cookies, cakes, or even candy! Punch a design from a piece of **construction paper** using a favorite Christmas **paper punch.** Center paper with design punched out of it over a treat. Using a **flour sifter,** lightly sift **powdered sugar** over paper, then *very carefully* lift paper straight up.

## cd surprise!

Store a collection of holiday stickers in a decorated CD case. Cut **colorful paper** to fit the front and back of a **CD jewel case.** (You'll find blank cases at music stores.) Stick paper down with **double-sided tape,** or slip paper inside slots on case and hold with a dot of **craft glue.** Add **gems** or **sequins** to spine with glue. Decorate with stickers, paper cutouts, fabric, or other accents. Then fill case with **stickers.**

## jolly ring

Ring in the holidays with an easy bead band. String enough **beads** on a 10-inch piece of **elastic** to fit around your finger. Tie elastic in a knot to make a ring. String 1 bead on each end of the elastic to make dangles. Tie knots about $\frac{1}{2}$ inch from ring to keep beads in place. Trim excess elastic.

## jingle bells

Go dashing through the snow wearing tiny bells. Tie a **bell** to an **earring hook** with a short piece of thin **elastic.** Make a bow, and trim ends.

## kris kringle krunch

Make a merry mix of pretzels. With an adult's help, melt **white chocolate chips** on high in a **microwavable bowl,** stirring chocolate every 30 seconds until melted. Dip half a **pretzel** in chocolate, cover with **white sprinkles,** and put on **wax paper.** Add a few drops of **red food coloring** to melted chocolate, then repeat directions. Put the pretzels into the fridge until hard. Gift idea: Gently slip pretzels into a **cellophane bag,** and tie with a **ribbon.**

## band boxes

These sweet striped boxes will help you stretch your holiday budget. Create a **rubber band** pattern around a **cardboard box,** keeping the bands flat. Paint the lid. Let dry. Stretch rubber bands around the edge.

# care packages

**Give loved ones a lift with a pampering gift!**

**hint** Swirl two colors together with a toothpick.

## fa la la la lip gloss

Give the gift of sweet and shiny lips with glistening glosses in delicious flavors.

**1** Ask an adult to help you grate paraffin wax onto wax paper. Measure ¼ teaspoon grated wax into a resealable plastic bag. Add 1 teaspoon coconut oil, 1 teaspoon petroleum jelly, and 1 candy melt. Add ⅛ teaspoon oil-based candy flavoring if you like.

**2** Seal the bag and carefully put it in a bowl of hot tap water to melt ingredients (3 to 5 minutes). Change water if it cools. Use only hot tap water. **Never use a microwave or a stove to heat the mixture.**

**3** While you're waiting, wash a small container with soap and water. Dry completely. Remove bag from water. Working quickly, squish ingredients around in bag to mix.

**4** Clip off a tiny corner of bag and squeeze gloss into container. Let set for an hour, or put in refrigerator for 15 minutes. To make gloss last longer, apply with a cotton swab instead of your finger. If gloss changes color, odor, or texture, throw it away.

**hint** Add candy sprinkles or crushed peppermint before gloss sets. Stir with a toothpick.

## magical wands

 No matter what shape these wands have, they blow round bubbles! Ask an adult to cut the eraser off an **unsharpened pencil.** Working from a **spool of 20-gauge craft wire,** wrap wire end around pencil 3 times to make a coil. Remove pencil. Open coil, put a **marble** on top, and wrap wire around marble. Place end of pencil on marble, then continue wrapping to top. Add a second marble if you like. Form a shape, such as a star. Be sure it will fit inside a jar. (See "bubble wrap" on this page.) Bend wire around itself to close shape. Cut off extra wire with **jewelry pliers.** Make sure clipped wire doesn't stick out, or it will pop the bubble before you blow it.

## bubble wrap

Wrap bubble solution and wands with **ribbon** for a lovable bubble package. Fill a **wide-mouth jar** with ready-made bubble liquid or mix **liquid dish detergent** with **water.**

# beaded boxes

All that glitters will look glamorous on cardboard boxes. Carefully untie a **hank of small beads,** and tie 3 knots at the end of each strand. Clip off extra thread. For a **small cardboard box,** lightly draw a **pencil** line just below lid. Remove lid. Spread **craft glue** around bottom edge of box. Press strands of beads into glue, straightening rows as you work. Finish a strand, then start a new one where you stopped. Bead up to pencil line, then bead sides of the lid. Starting with a new strand on top, work from outside edge toward center. Trim extra beads. Let dry. For a **large box,** cover top and sides with **acrylic paint.** Let dry. Bead lid. Outline snowflakes with glue, then use **tweezers** to stick on each **bead.** Gift idea: Slip hair doodads inside boxes!

# seasonal soaps

Use cookie cutters to shape a sleigh full of soaps, made from supplies you can find at craft or health food stores.

**1** ✋ To make 1 to 2 soaps, lay **aluminum foil** square on counter. Put **cookie cutter** on foil. Ask an adult to cut 1 cup of **glycerin soap** into ½-inch pieces, put into **microwavable bowl,** and microwave for 15 seconds. Stir, then continue to heat, checking every 5 seconds until soap just melts. Do not overheat!

**2** Quickly add ¼ teaspoon **soap glitter** and a few drops of **soap scent,** and stir. If soap hardens, reheat for a few seconds. Let a skin form, push it aside, and **spoon** a thin layer of soap into cookie cutter to make a seal. Press down on cookie cutter a few minutes while soap sets.

**3** Spoon or pour more soap into cookie cutter until it's nearly full. Let sit 2 hours. To ease release, place in freezer for a few minutes. Break off any soap around edges, then push soap out.

**hint** Melt different colors of glycerine soap together. For instance, mixing clear and green will make light green.

## holiday hair set

Reflect the holidays in a mirror and brush set. Outline a holiday design on **adhesive microbead paper.** Cut out design. Pull off paper's backing sheet, stick it on back of a **brush** and **mirror,** then pull off top sheet. Place item over a **rimmed cookie sheet,** and spoon on **microbeads.** Tap off excess beads. For a stronger hold, use a small **paintbrush** to cover beads with **craft glue.** Let dry.

## st. nick slippers

Bells will be ringing when you wear this pair of slippers. Slip a **threaded needle** through a **jingle bell** loop, then push needle through a fluffy **slipper** and back through to bell. Repeat a few times, and tie a knot. Sew bells around the top edges of both slippers.

# sparkle and shine

Let your spirit show with gifts that glow.

## snowflake string

Send snowflakes floating through the air. Stretch out a colorful **cord** on floor. String **beads** along cord. (Use a cord that just fits through hole in beads.) If beads slip, add a dot of **glue.** Make **paper** snowflakes with a **large paper punch,** and glue back-to-back between beads.

## row of rings

Link shiny circles together without tape or glue! Fold pretty **paper** in half. Place **tape roll** on paper so that tape edge touches folded paper edge. Trace inner and outer circles, and cut them out—but leave folded edge uncut! Repeat about 20 times. To link circles, unfold one, squeeze it so it can slip through hole of another folded circle, refold, and continue with remaining circles.

## paper bead chain

Deck the halls with shining paper bead chains! Draw a long triangle on **metallic paper,** and cut out as shown. Curl triangle tightly around a **knitting needle** or paintbrush handle. Add a drop of **glue** to end. Let dry 1 minute before removing needle or brush. Dry completely. Repeat to fill desired **cord** length. Add **regular beads** or **charms** if you'd like.

# princess purses

Tote your treasures in a sparkling bag! Use these stitching tips to get you started.

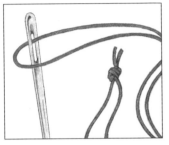

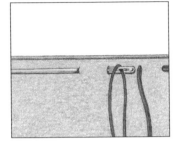

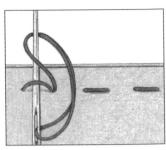

**Threading needle:** Pass 24-inch piece of thread through needle. Make ends even. Tie knot.

**Straight stitch:** Send point of needle down through both pieces of fabric and back up before pulling thread through.

**Knot:** Push needle down through fabric. Bring needle back up at start of stitch. To knot, slide needle under stitch and loop thread around as shown. Pull tight.

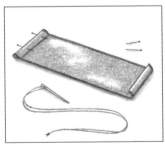

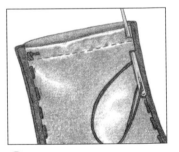

**1** Start with 8-inch piece of **2½-inch-wide (or wider) wire ribbon.** Lay ribbon flat on table, and fold in each cut edge ¼ inch. Keep edges in place with **pins.**

**2** Straight stitch along one edge as shown. Knot thread and trim ends with **scissors.** Repeat along other edge. Remove pins.

**3** Fold ribbon in half, with right side out. Straight stitch one side close to wire. Knot thread and trim ends. Repeat along other side. Sew on **thin ribbon** or **cord** strap.

**hint** Use beads for extra sparkle! Add a small bead on each stitch, or use beading thread to sew on a string of beads for a handle.

**hint** Tiny stitches look best, but they also take lots of practice. Try sewing a scrap of cloth or ribbon before you start your project.

## "oh, tannenbaum"

Design earrings to look like star-topped trees with boughs of beads! Curl a 9-inch piece of **34-gauge craft wire** around a **cake decorating tip** or fat pencil tip. Make a loop at top. Slide **star bead** along wire, then add **seed beads.** Put a dot of **glue** on wire end before adding last bead. Let dry. Adjust shape. Attach **earring wire.** Make a pair.

## festive frame

Create a frame as unique as you are! Lightly outline a design on a piece of **adhesive microbead paper** with a **pencil.** Cut out design with s**cissors** and stick it to **frame.** Remove backing sheet, hold frame over a **rimmed cookie sheet,** and spoon **microbeads** over adhesive paper. Tap off excess beads. Apply a thin layer of **craft glue** over beads with small **paintbrush.** Let dry.

## angel kisses

These celestial cuties start with a **Hershey's Kiss! Paint** a piece of **bow-tie pasta** for wings and a short piece of **spaghetti** and a **pasta ring** for a halo. Let dry. Glue pasta ring to top of spaghetti. Let dry. Cut a **mini marshmallow** in half with **scissors.** Draw a face on a half with a **marker. Glue** face on top of Kiss and wings on back. Attach pasta hair. Let dry. Stick halo into top of head. For decoration only (don't eat).

## gifts to glow

Make the holidays merry and bright with sparkling votive holders. Cover top edge of a **small glass flowerpot** with **microbead tape.** Working over a **rimmed cookie sheet,** spoon **microbeads** over tape. Roll edge in beads to fill in gaps.

33

## string ornaments

Dress up string in fancy holiday glitters.

**1** Fill a **small bowl** a third full with **craft glue.** Stir in **water** until glue is like cream. Blow up **small balloon** to size of golf ball, and tie off. Cut 2 inches from a **ball of cotton yarn.** Soak yarn in glue, and wrap it around balloon knot.

**2** Pull off a few yards of yarn from ball, but do not cut it. Drop yarn in glue mix, let soak, then wrap it around balloon. Add more glue-soaked yarn to balloon until it is covered in a web. Cut yarn, tucking end under web.

**3** Tie dry piece of yarn on knot to hang ball. Put **news-paper** under ball. In 1 hour, lay down **wax paper,** and sprinkle **glitter** over ball. Let dry overnight. Pop balloon, and gently pull it out through knot hole. Tie on a **ribbon.**

## tissue balls

Paper the tree with candy-colored bulbs.

**1** 🤚 For 2 bulbs, mix 1 tablespoon **wheat starch** (found at art stores) and 5 tablespoons **water** in **microwavable bowl.** With an adult's help, **microwave** on high for 20 seconds, stir, heat 10 seconds, stir, then heat 10 seconds more.

**2** Blow up **water balloon** to baseball size. Cut **tissue paper** into 1-by-4-inch strips. Use a **paintbrush** to cover balloon in paste. Lay strips on balloon, and paint paste over them. Overlap 2 or 3 layers of strips. Sprinkle **clear fine glitter** over bulbs.

**3** **Clothespin** balloon knot to a **string** and hang. Slip **newspapers** underneath. Let dry for 1 to 2 days. Unpin balloon, pop it, then gently remove it through knot area. Dip tissue paper square in paste and cover hole. Glue on **ribbon.** Let dry.

## star shine

Get wired for the holidays making sparkling star ornaments! Attach a ribbon to hang stars on a tree, above a window, or over a doorway.

**1** Using **pliers,** bend a 20-inch piece of **20-gauge wire** into a zigzag. Make first bend 3 inches from wire end. Add 8 more bends 1½ inches apart. Don't make bends too sharp or wire might break.

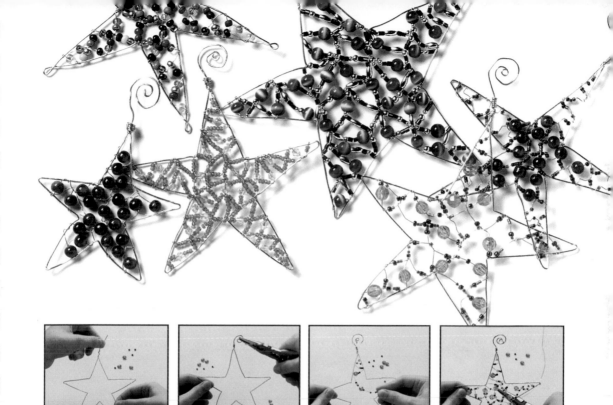

**2** Bring both ends of wire around so they crisscross at top. Tightly twist ends together to make a star frame. Be careful of sharp ends of wire.

**3** Twist one end of wire closed completely. Pinch other end with pliers and turn to form a spiral shape. To adjust star, bend wire with your fingers.

**4** Wind end of **26-gauge wire** around spiral base until secure. Slide **beads** on wire. Extend wire and attach to another side of star frame. Wrap wire at least twice around frame to secure.

**5** Place more beads on wire and continue to wind wire in random pattern, adding beads as you go. Finally, wind remaining wire around frame until secure, and trim excess. Tie on **ribbon.**

# frosty fun

**Snow and ice make Christmas twice as nice.**

# snowmints

These melt-in-your-mouth mints will tickle your taste buds!

**1** Wash hands. In a **bowl,** mix together with a **fork** 1 tablespoon **softened butter** (do not use margarine), 1 tablespoon **light corn syrup,** ⅛ teaspoon **salt,** and ½ teaspoon **mint extract.** Gradually add 1 cup **powdered sugar.** When dough becomes too stiff to stir, knead with hands.

**2** Make 12 snowmen with ¾ of dough by forming 2 or 3 marble-size balls for each one. Stack balls on **wax paper** to make bodies. Divide rest of dough in half. Knead 1 drop blue **food coloring** into one half. Wash hands. Knead 1 drop red and 2 drops yellow food coloring into other half.

**3** Wash hands. For each snowman, press on **candy sprinkles** for mouth, eyes, and buttons. Form a scarf, hat, earmuffs, and nose out of colored dough. Press features in place. Store in refrigerator.

## warm mittens

Celebrate the snow with mitten earrings made from paper clay. Knead **paper clay,** then roll it into ⅛-inch sheet between 2 pieces of **plastic wrap.** Trace mitten pattern from page 63 on **paper.** Cut mittens from paper, lay them on clay, and use a **toothpick** to cut around them. Wet fingertips to smooth edges. Add cuff details with toothpick. Insert a **jewelry finding loop.** Let dry for 2 days. **Paint** front of mitten, let dry 30 minutes, then paint back. Repeat with second coat. Attach **earring wires** to findings.

## santa's elf

Keep a holiday helper hanging around! Roll **paper clay** into a small ball, then shape it into a teardrop. Roll a rope shape, flatten it against hat for fur trim, then poke "fur" with a **toothpick** to add texture. Insert a **jewelry finding loop,** string on a **cord,** and hang to dry for 3 days. Add 2 coats of **paint.** (Let dry between coats.) Draw face with **waterproof markers.** Paint **glitter glue** on fur. Let dry.

# let-it-snow globes

Carry the snow wherever you go in a miniature snow globe pendant!

**1** Look for **glass necklace bottles with stoppers** at craft stores. Make bears, gifts, snowmen, or other shapes from **Fimo clay.** Be sure shapes will fit inside bottle. (Use shortest baking time on package directions.) Let cool. Color with **acrylic paint.**

**2** Ask an adult to squeeze **waterproof glue** onto bottom of clay object. Stick object onto bottle bottom with **tweezers.** Let dry for 1 day. In a **teacup,** mix $\frac{1}{4}$ cup **distilled water** with 2 teaspoons liquid **glycerin** (available at pharmacies and craft stores). Stir, then spoon mixture into bottles or use an old eyedropper.

**3** Sprinkle in **metallic glitter,** and stir with a **toothpick** to separate pieces. Press on stopper. If glitter falls too quickly, add more glycerin, and stir again. If there's too much glitter, pour out mixture and try again. For a lasting seal, add glue to stopper.

**hint** For a globe that's simple and sweet, use metallic glitter shapes, glitter, and glycerin.

## ice ornaments

Birds will love these festive fruit ornaments when the days grow warmer. Pour water (distilled freezes clearest) into a **muffin tin** or small bowl. For a hanger, fold **craft wire** or **wire ribbon** in half, and twist ends. Bend hanger so it both rests in water and hangs over edge. Add **fruit**, such as pomegranate seeds, and carefully put container in freezer for 4 hours. For easy release, dip container in hot water. Straighten out wire, open loop slightly, and hang ornament outside.

## frosty drops

Slip snowman earrings inside a pouch for a cool surprise. Starting with a 9-inch piece of **24-gauge wire,** make a bottom circle. Add 2 twists. Shape a top circle. Add another twist. Bend a tiny top loop. Clip ends with **pliers.** Repeat. (For easy circles, wrap wire around different-sized pens.) Press earrings onto **wax paper,** and fill with **craft glue.** Drop **beads** into glue to decorate. For noses, color **toothpick** tips with a **marker.** Snip off tips with **scissors.** Let glue dry clear, then peel off wax paper. Tie on **ribbon** scarf. Attach **earring wires.**

## jack frost

Jack is back to send holiday greetings to loved ones. Cut a circle from **heavy white paper,** and draw a face on it with **colored pencils.** Cut a tall triangle, a narrow rectangle, and a small circle from **fleece** or **felt** to make hat. Snip edges of circle to make pompom. Glue all pieces to a **blank card.**

# merry marshmallows

Coat homemade marshmallows in candy cane dust for a treat that will bring you comfort and joy!

**1** 🖐 With an adult's help, combine 2 cups **granulated sugar,** 3 envelopes **unflavored gelatin,** and ⅛ teaspoon **salt** in a **saucepan.** Add 2 cups **water.** Stir over medium-low heat until sugar dissolves. Heat for 3 minutes more, remove from stove, and stir in 1 teaspoon **vanilla.**

**2** Pour mixture into large **mixing bowl.** Tie back hair, then with an adult's help, use an **electric mixer** to beat at high speed for 10 minutes or until mixture looks like thick marshmallow creme. Pour into buttered **13-by-9-inch pan.** Let cool.

**3** Heat **kitchen shears** and **mini star cookie cutter** in hot tap water. Cut marshmallows into strips with shears, and lay strips on **wax paper.** Cut stars from strips with cookie cutter. For coating, slip **candy canes** into a **resealable plastic bag.** Crush candy with a **rolling pin** until very fine. In another bag, mix together equal amounts of **powdered sugar** and candy. Add stars, and shake to coat.

## christmas coasters

Serve seasonal sippers on coasters
made from wrapping paper. To
make 4 coasters, cut ⅛-inch-thick
**cork sheets** into four 4-inch
squares with **scissors.** Cover
**wrapping paper** with **clear
contact paper,** and cut out
eight 4-inch squares. Stick paper
to cork with **heavy-duty double-
stick tape.** Glue **gems** around
edges with **jewel glue.** Let dry
overnight. Wipe coasters clean with
a damp cloth. Do not put in water.

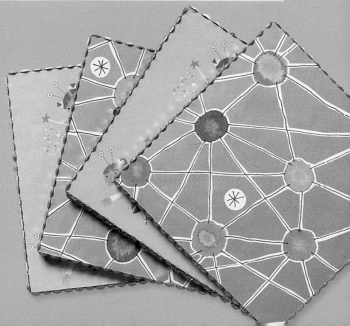

## polar pillows

Warm numb noses and cold cheeks with toasty mitten pillows. Enlarge mitten pattern from page 64 and trace it on **paper.** Cut out pattern, and **pin** it to 2 pieces of **fleece.** Cut around pattern with **scissors.** Place fabric together with right sides facing in. Sew edges, leaving cuff bottom open. (For sewing instructions, see page 30.) Turn pillow right-side out, and fill with **fiberfill** (sold at fabric stores). Fold cuff edges in. Stitch edges together with **needle and thread.** Apply **decorative trim** around cuff with **fabric glue.**

# it's a wrap!

**Get gifts ready to go with a bag, box, or bow!**

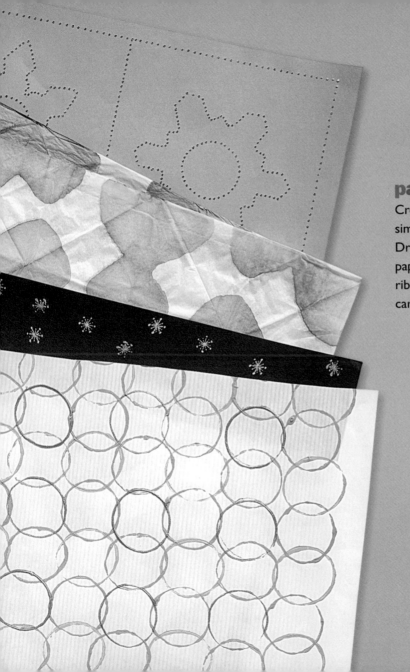

## paper play

Create luxurious wrap from simple household supplies! Dress up handmade wrapping paper with organza or silk ribbons. Create gift tags or cards to complete the package.

### tube trick

Pour **acrylic paint** on a **plastic plate**. Dip the end of a **paper towel tube** in paint, and press onto **plain wrapping paper**. Dip other end of tube in another color. Overlap circles. Let dry.

### seasonal stamps

Apply **acrylic paints** to holiday stamps with a **small paintbrush**, then press onto **plain wrapping paper**. Let dry.

### tie-dynamic!

Fold **tissue paper** into squares, rectangles, and triangles. In a **teacup**, mix ¼ cup **water** with 10 drops **food coloring**. Dip corners into coloring. Open flat to dry.

### pierced paper

Lightly draw a design on **plain wrapping paper**. Place paper over a carpet and carefully pierce around pattern with a **toothpick**. Leave a gap between holes.

## candy cones

Visions of sugarplums—and other sweets—will dance above heads after you hang these cones on tree boughs. Twirl a sheet of **vellum** or colored paper into a cone shape. **Glue** seam or use double-stick tape. Trim top. Run **glitter glue** along top edge and sprinkle with **glitter** or **microbeads** if you like. Decorate with other trims. Add a **cord,** ribbon, or beaded handle.

## tiny totes

Pack your bags with presents or party favors! Cover patterned side of a piece of **wrapping paper** with **clear contact paper.** Cut out rectangle strip, and fold in half. Trim top with **craft scissors.** Unfold strip, and press **double-stick tape** halfway along each side. Refold bag. Put holes in corners with a **paper punch.** Tie on a **cord** strap.

## tree charms

 Fill ornament boxes with tiny gifts, then hang them on the tree! Ask an adult to help you make a hole in the lid of a **small cardboard box.** Cover lid and box with **acrylic paint.** Let dry. Fold 12-inch piece of **ribbon** in half. Tie a knot, making a loop. Push loop up through hole in lid. Add ribbon to sides and bottom of box with **double-stick tape.** Fill box with tissue, add a gift, and slide down lid.

## celebration stars

For star treatment, wrap gifts in shining pyramids. **Glue 2 sheets of colored paper** together. Enlarge star pattern from page 63, cut out, then trace over paper. Carefully cut out star. Use **ruler** and end of **paintbrush handle** to score fold marks where triangles join bottom square. Make holes at the same place in all triangle points with a **hole punch,** and fold points up. Thread **ribbon** through holes, and tie.

## paper pockets

Make a pouch that's perfect for cards or goodies. Fold a long **paper** rectangle into thirds, shaping a pouch with a flap. Seal edges with **craft glue,** or make holes with **mini hole punch** and weave in **cord** or **ribbon**. Decorate with **stickers,** ribbon, or sprigs of evergreen. For blue pocket, trace pattern from page 62 onto vellum. Fold flaps on dotted lines, and overlap flaps to seal.

# secret santa stockings

Your pals will love these personalized socks!

Homespun style. Spread **fabric glue** over cuff and toe of a **knitted sock**. Press on **beads**. Let dry.

Sweet sock! Accent a **candy cane–colored sock** with **felt** trims, felt shapes, and **beads**.

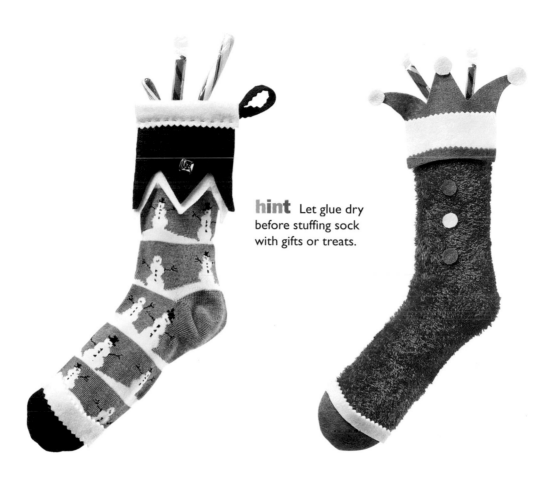

**hint** Let glue dry before stuffing sock with gifts or treats.

Winter blues! Cut **felt** with **scissors** and **craft scissors** and stick to cuff and toe of **seasonal sock** with **fabric glue**. Add a felt loop to top edge. Stitch on a silver **jingle bell**.

Puffy and playful. Crown a **chenille sock** with a jester cap cut from **felt**. Add felt buttons. Decorate toe.

## mini book necklace

Dress up a gift with a tag that can double as a necklace! Glue 2 pieces of **colored paper** to fit front and back of **hinge.** Glue a strip of paper to fit inside hinge. Decorate cover with **beads.** Let dry, then write a message inside. Poke hole in back cover through top screw hole. Fold **ribbon** in half to make a loop. Thread ribbon ends through hole, then through ribbon loop. Pull snug. Knot ends.

## christmas punch

Punch up presents with hand-made gift cards. Use **large** and **standard-size hole punches** to decorate cards. For ornament, **glue** a large **paper** circle onto a **blank card.** Cut a small white circle in half, and glue halves in place to make hanger and reflection. Draw a string with a **gel pen.** For snowflake, glue small circles on large circles, then glue onto a card.

# patterns

Patterns may be enlarged on a photocopy machine.

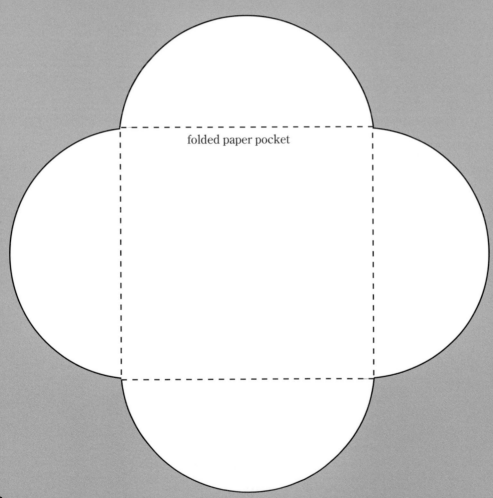

folded paper pocket

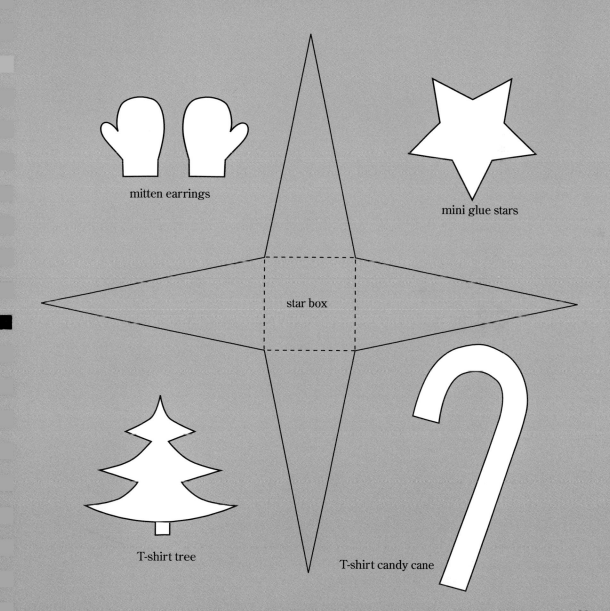

mitten earrings

mini glue stars

star box

T-shirt tree

T-shirt candy cane

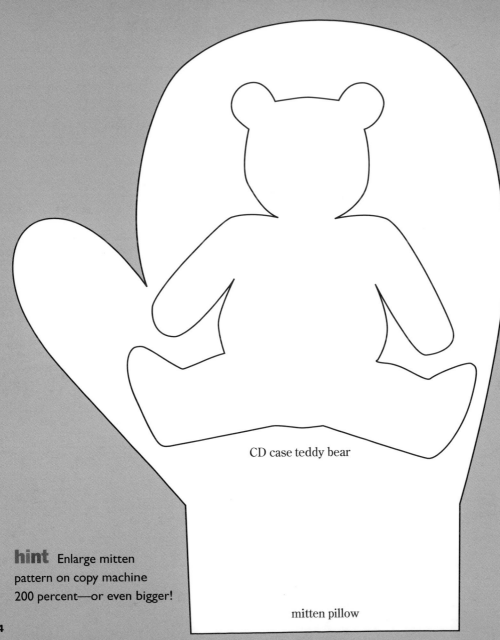

CD case teddy bear

mitten pillow

**hint** Enlarge mitten
pattern on copy machine
200 percent—or even bigger!